Action for Organizational Effectiveness Toolkit

This guide is aimed at corporates, business leaders, entrepreneurs, managers, executives, small business owners, and employees at all levels of the organization or stages of the business cycle concerned with the concept and nature of branding, from the dual perspectives of branding as a science and as an art . Each reference book in the series gives specific advice on how to complete a development task or solve a leadership, business, or organizational quandary.

SERIES EDITOR: Kennedy Mpezeni
EDITOR: Daniel Parirenyatwa
GRAPHIC DESIGN: Mehluli Hikwa

Printed in USA
ISBN: 978-0-9848943-1-4

Pangolin Corporate Training & Development
2 Tall Trees Lane
Borrowdale, Harare, Zimbabwe

Action for Organizational Effectiveness Toolkit

Brand It or Die!

Kennedy Mpezeni

Pangolin Corporate Training & Development®

To Our Valued Readers:

Personal and organizational developments are indispensable considerations and strategic initiatives in today's fast paced business economy. Survival necessitates the cultivation, refining, and development of pertinent knowledge, skills, and abilities (KSAs); you cannot afford to be stagnant. Through training, the person and the organization, along with the products and services offered acquire strategic advantage in an intensely fierce and competitive global market.

Pangolin Corporate Training and Development's (PCTD) series publications are designed to meet your current and long-term personal and organizational development needs. We identify training as a critical undertaking for any entity legitimately concerned about sustainable business success.

Our books can be used in formal training programs or in self-study, and provide the tools to advance and strengthen your organization's and its product's/service's position in the global business economy, and/or advance your career.

Our series publications assist you satisfy the market's need for innovation, originality, and demand for better skills, products, and services. We use our expertise to define, measure, and develop the capabilities needed to make organizations and individuals successful. These publications will help you improve customer connections and relationships, and increase organizational performance.

Delivering quality training product's that empower you is our primary objective.

Kennedy Mpezeni

Founder and Managing Partner

Pangolin Corporate Training & Development

Contents

Preface

The task of succinctly defining our contemporaneous global business economy could not be achieved in the absence of two defining words: competitive and dynamic. Today's business world is impetuously competitive and dynamic. Just a couple of decades ago businesses could plan and execute their strategies over a period of years, and not be overly concerned about having to modify them to ensure relevance and profitability. The 21st century presents a contra distinct reality. Our environment is characterized by expeditiously changing markets, globalization, shifting government policies, new technologies, and increasingly fickle consumer tastes, all of which make the task of branding more complex and critical.

Businesses are acutely cognizant of the need to pursue initiatives that promote sustainable growth and profitability, an objective grossly enhanced by effective branding. As a matter of fact no business can plan to survive and compete in the long-term without a well defined brand strategy. This book will help you develop and execute a winning brand strategy. It propounds strategic and operational brand principles and concepts. It unfolds the fallacious myth that portrays branding as the sole responsibility of a designated few subject matter experts, demonstrating that an integrated, holistic, and inclusive approach to the discipline will increase revenue and brand equity if done consistently and coherently. The development and execution of brand strategy is the responsibility of the entire organization. Branding has to be viewed as an integral and indispensable facet of overall business strategy. It would be detrimental to perceive branding as assuming secondary status, and as not being critical in the business scheme of things. Not only is branding critical but it is the difference between life and death. Since a strong brand has a significant impact on how your company, product, or service is perceived it makes building a strong brand critical to business success.

This book is written for you the Entrepreneur, career Professional, Corporate Executive, Small Business Owner, those in the business startup phase, and those contemplating starting a business venture. Inside you will be challenged to think with congruent construction and will find pragmatic tips on how to define, design, and implement an effective and winning brand strategy. When you have completed reading this book you will be confident in being the architect of a superior brand that will woo the hearts and minds of your customers. Branding is the process of creating and managing the big idea that summarizes all that your company, product, or service wants to stand for. Brand It Or Die, will inform you on how to align business and brand strategy which is the product of narrowing brand focus, great leadership, dedicated and valued employees, customer loyalty, and a strategic plan.

Good luck and remember, Brand It or Die!

Foreword

This booklet provides a panoramic view on the nature, discourse, and expression of branding. Its basic purpose is to highlight in a provocative idiosyncrasy the personality of branding, demonstrate the importance and need for businesses to give deliberate thought to the art and science of branding, to expound the fundamental precepts that constitute branding, and to encourage debate within businesses and among individuals concerned about the subject matter.

The primary, objective of the thoughts contained within this booklet are directed towards:

1. The revitalization and rejuvenation of existing brands
2. Providing a paradigm and critical concepts to be considered when creating a new brand
3. Effective management and optimization of results in the brand development process
4. Increasing brand competitiveness and reducing threats posed by new entrants
5. Assisting businesses deliver tangible and intangible value for their customers
6. Improving product and service image, hence increasing sales

There is an intensifying war in the marketplace as brands compete and wage war for customers. This has seen firms pouring huge sums of money into building strong, recognized, and accepted brands with an expanding loyal customer base. This warfare has caused business entities to reconsider their brand positioning, branding, and brand management strategies. Companies have learned either proactively or reactively that the concept of branding requires due diligence and continuous attention, causing them to innovate and think creatively with regards to strategy execution in managing their brand/s and the perceptions that emanate from this process.

Kennedy Mpezeni

Introduction

As the title suggests; Brand it or Die. Only two options exist, there is no neutral ground, it is an either or state of affairs. A pragmatic and logical approach suggests that the only choice is to *brand it*, and winning at this game requires a well thought out, constructed, and executed strategy. A strategy designed with particular intent and precision. Survival dictates this, or else you die. Branding will provide a strategic basis on which companies can find or consolidate a foothold. Advertising and other marketplace communications are to be based on and emanate from a solid brand strategy, a strategy that will illuminate the one thing that will make your offering/s better, different or more relevant than the competition.

The existent global business economy demonstrates intense competition, domestic producers of goods and services are not only competing with fierce local competition but with global suppliers of a wide array of commodities and services that are aesthetically packaged and presented and many derive from entities with an existing strong brand reputation.

A well designed and executed brand strategy is potent, it is lethal as it engages your target customer on multiple levels (*emotional, psychological, intellectual, sociological and some would dare say spiritual*) influencing and causing them to perceive and accept the benefits derived from associating and using your brand. If carried out with clinical precision the consumer will opt for your brand over similar brands simply because they would have connected with your brand and its ideals.

Brands are established to foster long-term chained connections between a company and customer. Branding is not a gimmick, nor is it a passing fad. It is about addressing your customers perceived requirements. As more alternatives become available customers choose brands they can trust over products that offer similar value. A brand is a powerful tool. Luxurious brands like Gucci or Louis Vuitton are negatively affected by counterfeits sold by illegal vendors; those who purchase the product are aware of the dissimilarity of quality however they still make purchase decisions driven by the power of the brand. This also demonstrates that branding is crucial to increase perceived consumer value.

One major but not exclusive role of the brand is to create identity. The identity design is usually assembled within a set of guidelines, and these guidelines ensure that the identity of the company is kept coherent. The identity or corporate image of the company is made up of a plethora of devices; name, service level, logo, stationary, marketing collateral, products, services, packaging, apparel design, signage, and anything visual that represents the business.

A solid brand will deliver the following and acquire strategic advantage:

1. Confirm your businesses credibility
2. Deliver your message clearly and unambiguously
3. Connect your business to your target market emotionally
4. Motivate the buyer and consolidate user loyalty and customer retention
5. Create a greater perception of your offering/s with targeted audiences
6. Create a platform for marketing communication effectiveness
7. Make you less vulnerable to competitive marketing actions
8. Create greater brand extension opportunities
9. Enable greater marketing communication effectiveness
10. More appreciative customer response to price increases and decreases
11. Greater brand/product extension opportunities

Today's market is the territory of and belongs to the branded, the rest are left in the dust, lose significance and eventually become irrelevant and die.

What Is Branding?
This chapter will help you to:

1. Define branding
2. Identify what branding is
3. Understand the key principals of branding
4. Remove popular misconceptions about branding

The paradox associated with the task of defining branding is convoluted and simultaneously facile. A central component of this process is articulating the demand of clarifying what a brand is not. The misconceptions associated with branding have blossomed into myth transformed into '*truth*' making the process of defining branding, notoriously difficult. As a matter of fact prior to being able to accurately and adequately define branding, we need to demystify it and engage in a process of demythologization. A widely accepted misconception is that branding essentially has to do with company logos, letterheads, packaging design, and business cards. A logo is not your brand nor is it your identity, any suggestion alluding to that is mere fallacy and needs to be dispelled. Logo design, identity design, and branding all have different functions that combined form a perceived image for a business, product or service. While these are facets that represent the brand to define the branding process within the precincts of these variables is myopic and arrests the potential of your brand to the detriment of the organization, along with its product and service offerings, ultimately negatively impacting profitability.

Branding is more than corporate logos, and aesthetic and alluring packaging, it is more comprehensive than those subset activities or particular expressions. The branding process is deliberate and complex, demanding and requiring a taking into cognizance of a plethora of branding attributes and dynamics which then inculcate a holistic approach to branding in an endeavor to strategically position your brand in your selected target market. There are entities that believe that they are branded but in reality all they have is a collection of logos and collateral materials. Have you stopped to consider that you may not be reaping the true value of your brand potential if you adopt or maintain a limited characterization of branding?

Branding: A Definition

The goal of branding is simple but the process is complex. Branding is one of the most important aspects of any business; an effective brand strategy creates competitive advantage in increasingly competitive markets. A strong brand is invaluable as the battle for customers intensifies. But what exactly is branding?

A company's brand is what a satisfied customer remembers and relates to the positive or negative experiences. Branding is not just a marketing or corporate identity function, it is something that lives in every experience a customer has with the company.

Vincent Grimaldi defines branding as a, "...combination of attributes, communicated through a name, or a symbol that influences a thought-process in the mind of an audience and creates value..." From this it is evident that branding is deeply anchored in psycho-sociology, considering it encompasses tangible and intangible attributes, functional and emotional benefits. These attributes compose the beliefs that the brands audience recalls when they think about the brand in its context. This definition further illustrates that superior brands cannot be built exclusively from product or service.

From this definition we can deduce that a brand is about manifesting your core identity. Branding is about connecting with your customer in a profound manner. It is as simple and rudimentary as that. Branding is about getting recognition and acceptance in your selected market with your desired consumer. Logos, letterheads, packaging, etc. are just important symbols of branding, but branding transcends that in that it is concerned with engaging these symbols to economically achieve visibility, recognition, following, and reputation. Branding is about getting your prospects to perceive you as having the solution to their problem. Branding is what your customers think of you and say about you once they have transacted with you. Your brand is what your company stands for and what it is known for. It is your promise to your customer. The true value of your brand for the audience is in the promise that the product or service delivers.

Branding is the blend of art and science that manages associations between a brand and memories in the mind of the brand's audience. It involves focusing resources on selected tangible and intangible attributes to differentiate the brand in an attractive, meaningful, and compelling way for the targeted audience.

The goal of branding is simple but the process is complex. A brand is an end result. Branding is the process by which a brand comes to be. Branding is a process that gives a product, service, organization, or personality a unique identity and image such that it is positively and easily identifiable and distinct from the competition. Thus a brand is more like self-definition or expression, so if your staff cannot define your company adequately they cannot promote the brand.

4 Considerations When Branding

Cost: *the process of creating a strong brand presence results in design and marketing costs*

Impersonal: *be wary of not losing your personal image*

Fixed Image: *once your image is created it is difficult to change*

Timescale: *the process of creating a brand will usually take a long time*

Defining Your Brand
This chapter will help you to:

1. Understand the importance of defining your brand.
2. Help you develop strategies for defining your brand.
3. Assist you identify and remove barriers that can keep your brand from being successful
4. Employing brand definition as a strategy to construct a strong brand within your market.

It is impossible to express or articulate clearly that which you have not defined and yet in violation of this rudimentary principle firms attempt to express that which they have not elucidated. The purpose of defining your brand is that you then become empowered to enunciate with intelligibility, exactness, and meticulousness your identity and essence to your target demographic in easily recallable syntax. Wherever transactions occur, the concept of branding assumes relevance for individuals, organizations, products, and services. Effective branding is contingent upon the fundamentals of psycho-sociology and is founded upon comprehension of the way audience's memories process, store, and recall information. Not taking the required steps to defining your brand is synonymous with you burying your head in the sand and hoping for the best.

Why Define Your Brand? The Rational Behind Brand Definition

 If you do not figure out what your brand is the marketplace will figure it out for you. Your task is to define your brand and communicate this consistently to the marketplace. If you do one without the other you are back to the marketplace defining your brand. Mixed syntax gives birth to confusion, diffused focus, and ultimately brand degeneration which erodes profitability and threatens product, service, or company longevity.

The purpose of defining your brand is to shape your company image in the consumer's psyche and ensure that:

1. You create a positive image in the mind of the consumer that is relevant to their needs and is easily recallable.
2. You are communicating a focused message to attract new clients, who increasingly shop around for similar offerings.
3. Well defined brands have a greater chance of influencing buying decisions and shapes perceptions held by customers and prospects.
4. You can only achieve consistency in delivering your customer promise if your employees have clearly understood your brand and its, objectives, this only takes place with a well defined brand.

Brand Definition: The Genesis of Great Brands

It is impossible to adequately define your brand without having firstly defined your customer. Do not put the cart before the donkey and attempt to define your brand without clearly and unequivocally understanding your target customer demographic and their perception of value. Defining your brand begins with your customer and their realities. Brand definition then becomes the platform that births the organizational framework that systematically manages those customer-centric processes. It aims at gathering intelligence, allocating resources, and consistently delivering the brand promise over time at each customer contact. Don't define your brand without first defining your customer.

Your brand definition will serve as your measuring stick in evaluating any and all marketing materials and strategies. You may have an existing brand that you have defined that you may need to evaluate in order for you to know what's going on with your brand and identify whether you did a good job of characterization. Ask yourself these questions:

1. Do you know what your brand is? (*If you don't, then you definitely have a branding problem*).

2. Do you know what your brand is but you don't have a full pipeline of ideal clients? (*Then you either have not communicated your brand to your ideal clients or you're missing the marketing piece. Or your branding is all wrong for who you want to attract so you may need to go back to the branding drawing board*).

3. Do you have a brand but you keep hearing things like: "Wow, I didn't realize you did this." Or 'I thought you only did that, not this.' (*Then you have a brand communication and/or marketing problem or you've gotten away from your brand*).

4. And of course if you hear things like "I'm not sure what it is you do." Or "You're the best-kept secret" you clearly have a brand problem.

Defining your brand eliminates existing or potential misconceptions associated with your brand in your selected markets. Your brand's power lies in its ability to connect and focus on your customer. It is your brand's objective to secure the devotion of your target audience to attain your branding goals. To achieve this you must know your target market inside out.

This requires scrupulous market analysis. Generally a well defined brand is a robust and resilient brand which in turn attracts and retains clientele if properly promoted through a marketing system. Defining your market will help strengthen your brand's efficacy. Your market analysis will require that you ask the following questions:

1. Where is your target audience located?
2. What do they think about your current brand?
3. How will you attract them to your products or services?
4. What would you like them to think about your brand?
5. Who else is competing for their loyalty and devotion?
6. Are you targeting business or consumer sectors?

If you do not know what your core identity is it means that you never took the time to map it out, as a result your products or services may struggle to compete in the marketplace, the anomaly is that you think that you are branded but in reality you have a confused, conflicting, or non-existent brand. This is dangerous for your business and sends the wrong message to your consumer.

The process of defining your brand provides a platform for you to develop your brand proposition which is relevant to your target market.

Naming: Brand Definition Does Not Happen Without It

Naming is a division of branding it is inconceivable to speak of a brand without a name, do not be fooled, those no name brands have a name, no name is the name. Any composition of sounds or - can compose a name, and perhaps may be unique enough as to identify a product or service without ambiguity. However that is not enough to make it a brand. To become a brand a name has to be able to fit in an audience's memory in a way that will make the brand attributes recalled. A well chosen name can be as powerful as a one word commercial. Naming is especially critical for small businesses, which often lack the necessary marketing budgets to promote their brand effectively.

5 Critical Steps to Defining Your Brand

A strong brand is the goal of brand definition, and a powerful brand in turn means that you have a cogent reputation in the marketplace.

1) *What does your company specialize in? This will assist you to identify and establish brand positioning and values.*

2) *Describe the products and services you currently offer and define the qualities of these products and services. Design a plan that best highlights product features and creates an image that appeals to a targeted segment (determines the best method for reaching audience). The goal of this plan is to grow and sustain brand equity.*

3) *Characterize the core values of these products and services. Are they aligned with the core values of your company?*

4) *What types of people do your products and services attract? Collect and analyze data identifying customers with wants and needs. This is done in order to measure and interpret brand performance.*

5) *What does your target audience think about your current brand? Determine boundaries in accordance with strategy. Determine most useful variables, this will assist you better plan and implement brand marketing programs.*

Benefits of Brand Definition

Powerful brands are grounded in authenticity and relevance which is preceded by brand definition. Your business success is directly proportional to how well you acknowledge what your customers really want and how diligently you apply your company's strengths, values, passions, and vision to satisfying that need, perceived and real. You define your brand in order to create a compelling personality, and it occurs prior to building your brand.

Defining your brand can assist you determine principal barriers that you may come into contact with. These barriers are also known as market conditions that can keep your product or service from achieving success. These barriers are*; competition, timing, financing, location,* and *lack of demand*.

Defining your brand will assist you create your brand identity, your brand identity will be repeatedly communicated, in multiple ways with frequency and consistency throughout the life of your business. By defining your brand you create the foundation for all other components to build on. Your brand definition will serve as a necessary stick in evaluating any and all marketing materials and strategies. Therefore; *define your brand.*

Brand Building: 7 Critical Considerations

This chapter will help you to:

1. Apply the 7 components of brand building to your brand
2. Identify and remove obstacles to efficaciously building your brand
3. Assist you build and develop a strong reputable brand

Adapted from Professor David Jobber: Seven Main Factors in Building Successful Brands

With the task of defining your brand behind you, your efforts can now be expended on an equally important aspect of branding, *brand building*. Powerful brands emanate from or are constructed upon the foundation of 7 generally accepted and agreed components:

i. **Quality**

    Quality is a vital ingredient of a good brand. Peter F. Drucker asserts that, "...quality in a product or service is not what the supplier puts in. It is what the customer gets out and is willing to pay for. A product is not quality because it is hard to make and costs a lot of money, as manufacturers typically believe. Customers pay only for what is of use to them and gives them value. Nothing else constitutes quality." Research confirms that, statistically, higher quality brands achieve a higher market share and higher profitability than their inferior competitors.

ii. **Positioning**

    Positioning is about the locus a brand occupies in a market and in the minds of consumers. Stalwart brands have a lucid, often unique position in the intended market. Positioning can be achieved through several means, including brand name, image, service standards, product guarantees, packaging and the way in which it is delivered. In fact, successful positioning usually requires a combination of these things.

iii. **Repositioning**

    Repositioning, often referred to as rebranding, occurs when a brand tries to change its market position to reflect a change in consumer tastes. This is often required when a brand has become tired, perhaps because its original market has matured or has gone into decline.

iv.   Communications

Communications also play a key role in building a successful brand. We suggested that brand positioning is essentially about customer perceptions – with the objective to build a clearly defined position in the minds of the target audience. All elements of the promotional mix need to be used to develop and sustain customer perceptions. Initially, the challenge is to build awareness, then to develop the brand personality and reinforce the perception.

v.   First Mover Advantage

Business strategists often talk about first-mover advantage. In terms of brand development, by "first-mover" they mean that it is possible for the first successful brand in a market to create a clear positioning in the minds of target customers before the competition enters the market. However, being first into a market does not necessarily guarantee long-term success. Competitors drawn to the high growth and profit potential demonstrated by the "market-mover" will enter the market and copy the best elements of the leader's brand.

vi.   Long-Term Perspective

This leads onto another important factor in brand-building: the need to invest in the brand over the long-term. Building customer awareness, communicating the brand's message and creating customer loyalty takes time. This means that management must "invest" in a brand, at the expense of short-term profitability.

vii. Internal Marketing

Finally, management should ensure that the brand is marketed "internally" as well as "externally". By this we mean that the whole business should understand the brand values and positioning. This is particularly important in service businesses where a critical part of the brand value is the type and quality of service that a customer receives.

Brand strategy will further entail the careful selection of elements fundamental to effective brand building. They include, but are not limited to, brand marks and logos, color and design systems, sounds, characters, URLs, taglines, and web design.

Developing Your Brand Strategy

This chapter will help you to:

1. Understand the importance of brand strategy
2. Develop your brand strategy
3. Create strategic brand advantage.
4. Understanding the critical success factors of your brand strategy.
5. Defining strategies to capitalize on strengths and market opportunities.

> The "Cheshire Puss", she [Alice] began..."would you tell me, please, which way
> I ought to go from here?"
> "That depends a good deal on where you want to get to," said the Cat.
> Lewis Carroll – Alice in Wonderland

The ultimate goal of brand strategy is to capture the hearts and minds of customers, and gradually lead them to the loyalty levels that produce brand equity. A good brand is nothing without the right strategy and a good strategy is nothing without the right brand. Your brand strategy must match your organizational core competencies and internal capacity to deliver upon your brand value proposition. Your brand loses equity, influence, and becomes obsolete when there is disequilibrium in existence between those two critical variables.

At the core of brand strategy is the generation of a plan that outlines how the company will create value for the customer, this can only be accomplished by knowing the customer's definition of value, and building upon brand strengths in a manner that synchronizes the outcome with the customer's perception of value. Strategy provides a foundation for development of brand building programs and typically includes brand objectives, consistent brand name and identifying a system, target audience, positioning, key communications messages, and prioritization of brand touch points.

Brand Vision

The cultivation of brand strategy requires the delineating of a brand vision that relates the company's mission to its desired perceptions. This vision provides a strategic basis for the articulation of a specific, relevant, and memorable brand position. Strategy and vision are inseparable. Great brands oscillate around the axis of courageous, audacious, and bold vision. Positioning becomes the aspect of the vision to be communicated to each target audience in order to create the desired perception. A differentiating and compelling positioning is fundamental to any effective communications effort. This work will follow directly from the stakeholder research and be designed to address the strengths, weaknesses, discovered through the audit. Once a brand vision and positioning are articulated, a creative team can evaluate which elements identified in the brand inventory are appropriate to the new strategy, which need to be replaced, and what new elements can be employed to further bring the brand to life, make it more robust, and consolidate it.

Your vision should force you to stretch your competencies beyond the confines of your comfort zone. You may not have the capacity to execute the totality of your strategic vision for your brand but you would have defined targets to grow towards. These strategic goals should regulate your business activity and dictate how you allocate and deploy your resources. By doing this you avoid being trapped in a labyrinth of confusion caused by activities competing for your attention and resources. Gone are the days when your, corporate or brand strategy could be more long term focused and almost stagnant. Today's business economy has no room for stagnancy. The paradox of brand strategy is that it has to be consistent and yet dynamic, dynamism is more about application of the same message in contexts undergoing transmutations. Your brand strategy has to be, at minimum, as dynamic as the environment it finds itself in, it can do this in two possible ways by evolving with the environment or by causing the environment to transform by creating markets for its brands. Failure to do so will kill your brand.

Brand Strategy

A strategic basis is critical in regards to the creation of a foothold, for example advertising and marketing activities are to be based on a solid brand strategy. A main advantage derived from a well defined brand strategy is that it will illuminate, the "one thing" that makes the brand offerings better or different or more relevant than the competition.

Think of strategy as the composition of those competitive moves, combination of tactics, and business approaches designed to transport your brand from where it is to where you need to be taking it, which is reaching customers, competing successfully, and achieving expressed metrics. Businesses use these moves to reach customers, compete successfully, and achieve organizational objectives. Successful organizations know that brand strategy is not stagnant; it is an emergent process that focuses on competitive advantage, competitive differentiation, sustainable advantage, and barriers to entry. Crafting a winning brand strategy is challenging enough even when you have articulated your brand promise, and is probably impossible if you haven't. In essence brand strategy is about taking your brand from where it is to where it needs or where the vision dictates it should be.

Like most dimensions of branding brand strategy commences with top notch research, it is not exempt. It is not possible to develop your brand strategy without first having understood some dynamics that facilitate the construction of brand strategy. These facets have already been discussed in preceding chapters but it is important to take note that those steps precede brand strategy cultivation, they give your brand strategy a point of reference, and context thereby legitimizing or authenticating your brand strategy.

What are your brand objectives?

Brand Strategy Decisions

Brand strategy decisions involve brand positioning, brand differentiation, brand name selection, brand sponsorship, and brand development:

Brand Positioning: positioning a brand clearly in the target customer's minds, based on brand attributes, benefits, beliefs, and values.

Brand Differentiation: better physical attributes better value, new segments, or underserved markets.

Brand Name Selection: a good name greatly adds to the product's success hence a name should be carefully selected and protected.

Brand Sponsorship: manufacturer's have four options—: manufacturer's brand, private brand, licensed brand, or co-brand.

Brand Development: a company has four options – Line extensions (variations of existing product) Brand extensions (existing brand extended to new products) Multi-brands (new brands in the same product category) and New brands.

Identify and cultivate opportunities to educate your target demographic on the benefits associated with selecting your brand over other brands.

Crucial Dynamics of Brand Strategy

The components to an effective brand strategy consider three crucial dynamics.

The first consideration tackles your company brand direction as played out in your customer experience, new or existing product and service development, company activities, and budget.

The second consideration grapples with the external environment, which pays due attention to economic cycles, competitive threats, regulatory threats, and industry threats.

Lastly, strategy has to take seriously the issues of Return-On-Investment (ROI) and improvement initiatives; this generates a conscious paradigm of how the organization will handle implementation, benchmarking, contingencies, feedback, and fine-tuning.

When Crafting Strategy Think Hearts & Minds First, Then Money later

Creating a positive emotional association in your market for your product or service is a key. It can create want and desire by the mere mention of your brand, product, or service name. Positive emotional associations are built over time through good branding practice and a time tested relationship between you and your customer based on intrigue, trust, understanding, and support. Your brand strategy should be crafted around emotional benefits. To do this, list the features and benefits of your offerings (features are attributes such as color, configuration, and the benefit, is what the feature does for the customer). Then you should determine which benefits are most important for each customer segment. Once you have done that, identify which benefits are emotional, and then look at the emotional benefits and boil them down to one thing that a customer should think of when they think of you.

To create a brand promise that creates such an emotional attachment it must:

i. Be grounded in the brands core values
ii. Clearly and relevantly engage your target market
iii. Create a positive emotional attachment beyond just being good
iv. Be repeated internally and externally within your organization
v. Adapt to the business environment
vi. Be continually reinforced
vii. Be consistent across marketing and advertising mediums
viii. Be known and echoed by business partners

Staff Right To Brand Right: Human Resource Management (HRM) and Brand Strategy

The truth is branding starts with your employees. If they are failing to accurately reflect your brand it is likely, that they are diminishing your marketing efforts. You cannot separate brand strategy from the people who execute the strategy (not even for analytical purposes). Powerful brands are not birthed in a lacuna but are the result of a collective effort of a team of individuals. In fact it is impossible to build and manage a strong brand without the right people on your team to define your brand and determine your brand strategy.

Great brands begin with great people. As much as you cannot have a powerful brand without the right people on board you cannot define your brand strategy nor let alone execute it without the right team members. In short, after you have defined the vision for your brand start with the people to execute and deliver your brand value proposition (some proponents argue that you should start with the people before you define the vision, then allow the vision formulation process be collective).

HRM should ensure that all of the large or small actions people take everyday throughout the organization, fall in line with brand strategy. This requires that employees should become familiar and knowledgeable with the company's brand strategy. HRM should convert and translate the brand promise into brand behaviors. For that to be effective The HRM function should help identify the particular behaviors required to deliver the promise, however identification is elementary, the behaviors have to be inculcated and breathed in the very life and actions of the totality of the organization. After operationalizing the brand promise, the next step is to make sure training and development, performance appraisal and management systems are existent, supported, and expressed.

A consequence of brand strategy is that it gives all staff something clear to aim for. A good way of explaining brand strategy is by painting an inspiring vision of a hypothetical future, 'if we do these things by 2015 we will look like this.'

Steps to Achieving Consistency between Human Capital and Brand Strategy

Synchronize Your Brand Personality, Values, & Corporate Culture: the different functional areas of your business should be working closely together to ensure that the common values of your company internally and externally are in sync.

Get Your Employees Behind Your Brand: align your criteria for recruiting and rewarding employees with the criteria of the brand value. Look for the right skills and aptitude that will represent your brand promise effectively.

Reinforce & Repeatedly Explain Brand Values & Behavior: use your internal communication to reinforce and explain the values and behavior that reflect your brand promise. Continuously do this until it becomes second nature.

Your people must be well trained in articulating and delivering on your brand particularly for service oriented organizations. A brand's functional values have become harder to sustain, and emotional values play an increasingly important role, hence the attitudes and behaviors of staff have become critical brand differentiators. When employees don't deliver the brand, it can be the kiss of death for your business. Your employees are the face of your brand. TRAINING

Brand Strategy Requires Brand Integration

Resist the temptation to fall into the trap of isolating brand strategy to the activities and sole responsibility of the marketing department. Brand strategy development and implementation is not the sole responsibility of the marketing department, just as profitability is not the sole responsibility of the finance department. Effective brand strategy is not built in isolation, it is integrated. It must have a close relationship with the overall business strategy and goals. Brand strategy is part of business strategy, it comes before some components and after some others, but it must have a definite, concrete, and symbiotic relationship with business strategy and goals.

Integrated branding is the process of revealing the brand promise, then aligning the entire organization to deliver the promise. Living the integrated brand is the road to long-term business success and sustainability. The goal of integrated branding is to create a company that consistently and carefully orchestrates and delivers to the consumers the initial brand promise. If your company has integrated its brand, every employee from the top down knows what the company is good at, its personality and its key promise to the consumers.

When employees are living an integrated brand, they can:

i. *Make a decision faster and smarter.*
ii. *Consistently act in a way customers appreciate.*
iii. *Design products and services that emphasize the company's key promise.*
iv. *Consistently act to increase the company's differentiation.*
v. *Hire the type of people and create a work environment that reflects the company's values.*
vi. *Budget the company's money in a way that builds the brand and reinforces key brand attributes.*

4 Key Success Factors in Attaining Brand Integration

i. **Senior Management Stewardship**
   Visible leadership will drive consistent behavior. Top managers must demonstrate that alignment is a high priority for the entire company through their comments to brand goals, values, and behaviors.

ii. **Aligning Business & Brand Strategy**
   Customer relationships fuel success. Brand strategy must foster loyalty based relationships by defining relevant, differentiated, and credible value proposition. This can be achieved by ensuring the product and/or service quality is consistent with your brand promise.

iii. **Responsibility & Accountability**
   Middle managers are, key to delivering the brand promise. This role is to infuse the operations with a practical commitment to living the brand. This protocol applies as much to "back office" functions as to sales and customer service.

iv. **On-going Performance Measurement & Feedback**
   What gets measured gets done. A coherent brand evaluation program with milestones, progress measures, and celebration of success is vital for sustaining the momentum of internal brand alignment.

Family Branding vs. Individual Branding Strategies

The greater a, company's brand equity, the greater the profitability that the company will use a family branding strategy rather than an individual branding strategy. This is because family branding allows them to leverage the equity accumulated in the core brand. Some of the aspects of brand equity include brand loyalty, awareness, association and perception of quality.

Execution of Brand Strategy

Brand management can be safely integrated at the very center of any organization as a means to driving its strategy and its culture in symbiosis with its internal and external environments. Your brand strategy is useless unless it is implemented. Brand delivery or the execution of brand strategy within the organization is effective when people feel ownership and empowered as they are more likely to take the process of delivery more seriously. Effectual brand delivery occurs through the mediums of culture and operations and this depends on ownership, commitment, and responsibility.

The effectual deployment of brand strategy authenticates your brand in the jungle that we call the market. Aligning your brand strategy comes from narrowing the brand focus, great leadership, dedicated and valued employees, customer loyalty, and a strategic plan. However the true strength and integrity of your brand strategy relies on and only becomes evident with great execution, a brand can only make a powerful statement if it inspires powerful execution that is constantly implemented across every touch point, which is inseparable from brand integration.

The truly integrated brand

Remember to make your brand strategy work you need to ensure the following is carried out:

1. Maximize the breadth of insights. Inform the brand from right across the business.
2. Clarify objectives and share widely
3. Ensure that the strategy is comprehensive and addresses many brand attributes
4. Integrate brand strategy and other parts of business planning
5. Wrap the brand strategy into a vision for the organization
6. Invest in delivery, resourcing, responsibility, and rewards

Brand Innovation and Creativity

Outthink outcompete outfox the competition

Innovation and creativity are the contemporary buzz words in our contemporary business environment. As a matter of fact mentioning them appears as though it were cliché. However it is sheer folly to underestimate their potency and bottom line impact.

5. Brand Repositioning

This chapter will help you to:

1. Identify effective approaches to brand repositioning
2. Construct a paradigm and rationale for pursuing brand repositioning

This particular sub-topic is of tremendous and particular relevance for brands competing in the current Zimbabwean context. It is critical due to the competitive pressures, new channels, and changing consumer needs. The last decade that witnessed the economic meltdown resulting in the absence of profitable sustainable economic activity removed incentives for brand management and development. As a result local firms lagged behind their foreign competitors, particularly in the manufacturing sector of the economy. Firms failed to invest in the necessary equipment or replace redundant and obsolete infrastructure, machinery, and technology that would consolidate a brands competitiveness and appeal within a 21st century environment. Likewise service delivery was also negatively implicated. Today's consumer is exposed and continues to be exposed to a plethora of brands, many of which are already household names, and are competitively positioned.

Brand Repositioning: A Definition

Brand repositioning, commonly referred to as *rebranding* refers to the process of redoing a company's services or products position in order to adapt to changes in the marketplace, this occurs or is prompted by the need to re-establish the value of the brand. The author prefers to utilize the term brand repositioning as opposed to rebranding as a consequence of what the terms suggest. The term rebranding is not inclusive of the reason why rebranding. Repositioning indicates acquiring new position for competitive advantage. It is imperative that prior to auctioning a repositioning strategy that thorough market research and analysis is carried out.

There are multiple reasons compelling firms to reconsider their brand positioning, however at the forefront of these reasons is *change*, the market is not static, but dynamic. Jack Welch, former CEO of General Electric put it succinctly when he said, "...you've got to be on the cutting edge of change, you can't simply maintain the status quo because somebody is always coming from another country with another product, or consumer taste changes, or the cost structure does, or there is a technology break through. If you are not fast and adaptable, you're vulnerable..."

Take note that the reason brand repositioning is carried out is in order to firmly plant the brand in the minds of your targeted customer demographic and improve overall market share. It is of paramount importance that you do not lose sight of that. Firm's fail to achieve these objectives as their goals outstrip their ability to deliver what is promised to their customer, or essentially to deliver on their value proposition. To mitigate the risk of failure it is imperative that you pursue a brand repositioning strategy that is eminently achievable and not just attractive and aesthetic.

Reasons Why Firms Consider Brand Repositioning

Local competition is global competition. In order to grow and prosper many companies are seeking business opportunities in global markets, by doing so they expand their markets and take advantage of economies of scale. The intensity and diversity of competition is arguably the number one reason why firms consider adopting and implementing a brand repositioning strategy. In order not to lose significance, to remain competitive, to maintain and/or increase market share, firms pursue brand repositioning strategies.

4 Reason's Firms Consider Repositioning Strategies

Change is the only constant in the marketplace and firms are constantly seeking ways to remain relevant and competitive, and maintaining a positive brand image. A firm can choose several positioning strategies, their choices include, strengthening the current position, repositioning, or attempting to reposition the competition, our focus is on repositioning.

1) When the first position is wrong.
2) When there is strong competition in the marketplace.
3) When the target consumer is to be changed.
4) To rebuild a brand's personality.

3 Steps to Ensure Brand Repositioning Success

Consultancy firm McKinsey and Company have identified and propounded upon 3 steps that can help ensure brand repositioning success.

a) *Ensure Relevance To A Customer's Frame of Reference*
b) *Secure The Customer's Permission For The Repositioning*
c) *Deliver On The Brand's New Promise*

a) *Ensuring relevance to a customer's frame of reference* is pivotal to, affecting a successful repositioning strategy, this ensures relevance to a customer's context this is the only way it will resonate with the customer. Study and understand the customer context. McKinsey asserts that it is necessary to look at a combination of customer attitudes and the situations in which the brand is used to obtain the most powerful customer insights. Capture not just the emotional and physical needs of the customer, but the dynamics of the situation in which these needs occur. Repositioning a brand too far from the customer's frame of reference creates confusion. Successful brands are culturally relevant, are in touch with ideas, issues, and sensibilities that influence their audiences decisions.

b) The succeeding step is to *secure the customer's permission for the repositioning*. In order to achieve this objective you have to recognize that permission amounts to a reasonable and logical extension of the brand in the customer's eyes. To do this effectively you have to leverage a brand's unique emotional benefits to carry customers from their current brand perception to their intended one. Securing permission is to claim the ground to which the brand aspires. Permission amounts to a reasonable and logical extension of the brand in the eyes of the customer, building a bridge that can carry customers from where they perceive your brand to be today to where you want to take it in the future.

c) The third and final step is to *ensure that the organization is ready to deliver on the brands new promise*. As you deliver on the brand promise you also want to communicate this to your customer. To achieve this you must identify the pathway of performance signals that will convince the customers of the new brand positioning. To internally support the new brand position it is imperative to develop product and service programs to ensure consistent performance on these signals. You will have to track and assess performance against customer signal prior to launching the new positioning. Ensure that what you say, is what you do, brand performance must live up to its promise.

Be cognizant of the fact that this is a process as opposed to an event it is prudent to adopt an interim positioning to establish credibility and performance prior to a comprehensive and complete rollout. Make sure approaches are in place to track and assess your performance against the customer signals prior to the formal launching of the new position, quality assurance procedures ensure that customers are not disappointed, or fail to have their expectations met. Caution should be taken in order to avoid falling into the trap of expressing your repositioning strategy as a mere communication or messaging framework by another name. Your brand repositioning strategy sits above these tactics to deliver the desired and intended consequence.

Your repositioning efforts should ensure a smooth transition from where your brand is to where you seek to take it.

Branding And Marketing

This chapter will help you to:

1. Identify the inseparableness that exists between branding and marketing
2. Utilize marketing techniques to gain competitive advantage

The true power of a brand lies in what customers have learned, felt, seen and/or heard and accepted about a brand resulting from their experiences over time. Branding and marketing ought to create confidence that consumers place in a brand over their competitors. Once created brands are communicated and positioned for the relevant audience in such a way that the brands characteristics match consumer expectations. An important intersection between branding and marketing is realized in their objective of influencing the cognitive processes of their target consumers. The benefits of successfully executing this cannot be overstated. To clarify, strong power in the mind can withstand lower buying power in the market as the inherent desire for the brand can overcome less favorable market conditions.

Intersections: Branding and Marketing

Outside the world of brand and marketing managers the purpose and role of marketing is not well understood and even fewer grasp the meaning of branding. Marketing and branding are central elements of any successful business. Branding is the foundation of marketing and inseparable from prudent business strategy. Marketing does not determine what a brand will be or how high its quality will be. It does determine how the product is perceived by the public, and it is best done when working from a position of strength, in other words, a strong brand can be more easily marketed, but that does not mean that every great brand will market itself. Nor does it mean that every successfully marketed brand is the best in the field.

What marketing does is to determine the proper audience for a brand and then deliver to that audience what it wants. The target demographic can be as narrow as 40 year old single mothers living in the low-density suburbs, or it can be literally anyone; that will depend upon the product. But once the demographic is identified, marketing professionals analyze it, make sure the characteristics of that demographic are compatible with the product, and then emphasize the strengths of the product. The strengths of the product are very specific they are the strengths that will cogently convey the personality the demographic wants to see in themselves. Marketing is the art of taking what already exists and making it more attractive to the public through branding and positioning techniques, advertising is what happens when marketing is already done.

Studies have demonstrated that companies that market their products or services without first completing the assignment of establishing their brand identities are not likely to achieve return on investment. Branding is one of the most misunderstood concepts in all of marketing, even among professionals. Branding is not advertising and it is not marketing or PR. Branding happens before all those. First create the brand and then raise awareness of it. To draw an analogy, marketing can be thought of as a toolbox containing branding, advertising, direct mail, market research, public relations, and other tools. Marketing represents the combination of methods organizations use to persuade their target audience toward some specified behavior such as sales.

Though branding is a facet of marketing it is a distinct and yet inseparable dimension. In the recent past the two dynamics have become more appreciative of the other. Modern marketing defines, develops, and delivers value to customers these are represented and expressed by the brand. Today, the question of utmost importance for most brands is how to satisfy people who have an almost endless choice reinforced by instant access to the global market. Marketing is not a battle of products it is a battle of perceptions. The power of the brand lies in what resides in the minds of customers, what they have learned about your brand, felt, seen, and heard about a brand as a result of their experiences over time.

The only way to ensure long-term profitability is to provide the customer with superior value. Your, customers willingness to pay is the ultimate test of value that has been created by your brand, brand equity in other words. Marketing's role is to translate the overarching business strategy into process performance that will ensure the highest possible sales to the most valuable customers. Branding by expressing the firm's values and image makes that connection with your customer. Market research sets the direction for the development of products, define the business by identifying market demands, trends, and customer preferences; the brand solidifies that connection with the customer (how).

Marketing your brand requires capital, capital impacts capacity by the amount of finances it makes available for brand marketing activity.

Make sure your marketing activity is relevant.

Your desired brand image impacts your brand communication strategy. A strong brand is not mutually exclusive from the manner by which you communicate your brand to your target demographic.

Brand Exposure

One of the responsibilities among marketing's plethora of activities is to create in relation to return the greatest level of brand exposure. Brand exposure is about creating and capitalizing on opportunities to communicate and make your brand visible to customers. The best branding becomes valueless if potential customers are not exposed to it. The process of creating a durable brand will require that you craft and optimize opportunities for maximum brand exposure.

There are four generally accepted and recognized methods that can be employed to expose potential customers and generate brand awareness and assist them remember your brand:

i. **Advertising:**

In today's business climate even the most secure brands need to advertise. The look of a television or print ad is as important as the message being delivered in print or dialogue. When a brand is being introduced it is important that the target audience be able to identify the brand and identify with the brand. Advertising does not create the identity but it does choose how to present the identity assists define the identity of the product and by extension its users.

The goal of advertising is to grab attention, create positive perceptions, and prompt a response while conveying information consumers will find relevant to their need. Brand advertising is at the heart of any business success.

It should be noted that advertising should always consider the type of business you are in and the targeted customer demographic you are trying to expose your brand and sell to. Advertising mediums that can be employed could include; magazines, newspapers, billboards, trade journals, radio, television, and the internet. This is the best way of exposing your brand since it reaches a great number of people. A downside is the expense factor advertising is expensive, particularly over a protracted period of time.

ii. **Public Relations:**

PR exposure can disseminate pertinent information about your brand to a wide pool of people through reliable mediums such as trade journals. PR is not as costly as advertising but results will diverge depending on the type of business you run. If you choose to carry out PR internally it will cost next to nothing but results are often pitiable especially in the absence of prior training and adequate knowledge. When choosing an external company make sure you establish their competence and experience to avoid wasting valuable resources.

iii. **Word of Mouth (WoM)**

Generally a satisfied customer will communicate their experience with your business to other people this can assist to spread your brand. The reverse is also true. Actually research indicates that an unsatisfied customer will usually tell more people than satisfied customers. WoM exposure does not cost anything and if it is positive it will help lodge your brand name and image in your potential customers mind. It is important to ask for WoM exposure, an example of this would be giving discounts for customer referrals. Advertising and promotions are other mechanisms that can encourage WoM, teaser advertising and competitions often make people talk about the advert and thus your brand.

iv. **Period of Establishment (PoE)**

You have no control over time and hence PoE as a form of exposure. Truly great brands are built over time, it takes years for a brand to become effective and permeate the social fabric. Consider the world's best brands and you will notice that a number have been established for over 50 years.

Creating and maintaining a strong brand presence involves design and marketing costs. A strong brand is memorable but it still requires people to be exposed to it and this requires a lot of PR and advertising over a long period of time.

Brand Equity: Beyond Brand Recognition

This chapter will help you to:

1. Extend beyond the limits of brand recognition in executing your brand strategy
2. Acquire a more comprehensive understanding of the concept of brand equity

Getting your brand recognized is important but is not an end in itself. Your organizational competencies have to stretch beyond brand recognition to brand acceptance, and brand loyalty, then and only then do you have brand equity. Even then if you do not remain relevant and innovative, consistently maintaining unswerving commitment to customer needs and wants, then your brand equity will last for only a season. There are volumes of meticulous and useful research on the subject of branding and branding recognition, but the real question is; now you have constructed the symbols that reflect your brand what is next? Your brand has attained visibility (*recognition*) – *what next?* Brand recognition is fundamental but is not an end within itself it exists to serve a greater purpose.

There are three critical areas of consideration that lie beyond brand recognition that entities have to deal with in order to reap the benefits of having cultivated recognition and realizing brand equity:

1. Brand Acceptance and Brand Loyalty
2. Brand Communication
3. Brand Innovation and Creativity

To a consumer your brand is synonymous with your company people build a relationship which is very personal to your brand not your company per se. The best brands build an emotional connection with consumers, leading to customer loyalty.

It is critical that you are cognizant of the fact that activities that you engage in, in order that your brand achieves recognition within the market are not sufficient enough. Brand recognition is not an end but can arguably be stated to be the commencement of your journey to achieve your objectives. Recognition addresses the need to distinguish your brand in a marketplace inundated with a plethora of brands. Recognition is the result of brand distinction. The reason you want brand recognition extends beyond awareness and into loyalty that translates to brand equity.

Brand Equity

Have you considered why brands are important to consumers? Brands are important to consumers because they provide information and remove risk and uncertainty. Uncertainty impacts the consumer in two ways. Firstly, it increases the risks of buying the brand and follow-on consumption experiences. Risk is higher for products and services that consumers must buy and experience in order to *"know"* the features or product attributes. If brand features or attributes can be learned easily before purchase, consumers would be more certain about them. Secondly, uncertainty causes consumers to invest more time and effort in making choices. They incur information costs, resulting in more information search and cognitive effort. Hence the role of brands in choices is to serve as "shorthand" to reduce perceived risk and lower information costs. The fundamental role of brands is to save consumers effort and time in making choices by helping to insure that future consumption experiences will be what consumers expect. Thus brand equity or value arises out of consumer choices, and brands cannot have value independently of consumer choices. That is brand equity exists only because brands increase the utility of products and/or services to the consumers who buy them.

A brand with strong brand equity is a very valuable asset, and a powerful brand has high brand equity. Brands have higher brand equity to the extent they have higher brand loyalty, name awareness, perceived quality, strong brand associations and other assets such as patents, trademarks, and channel relationships. Keller (2000) asserts that brand equity provides marketers with a strategic bridge from their past to their future. That means each dollar spent each year on marketing cannot be so much thought of as expenses, but investments in what consumers know, feel, recall, believe, and think about the brand.

Essentially brand equity has to do with the results that accrue to a product with its brand name in comparison to results that would be attained had the product not had the brand name. Well known brand names allow companies to charge premium prices. What really lies, at the root of this is consumer knowledge, acceptance, and loyalty. Brand equity increases financial value. Elements that can be included in the valuation of brand equity include changing market share, profit margins, consumer recognition of logos, and other visual elements, associations made by customers, consumer perceptions of quality, and other relevant brand values. Brand equity permits the brand to earn greater margins or volumes than a product or service would without the brand name, thus giving the brand a strong, sustainable, and differentiated edge over competitors. It is essential to note that brand equity is exhibited by the value a consumer places on a particular brand above that which would result from an otherwise identical product or service without the brands name; this alone contributes value to the offering.

The creation of brand equity is a strategic objective. There are 3 dimensions of brand equity. Manufacturers and retailers are interested in the strategic and cash flow implications of brand equity. Investors are primarily concerned with the financial value of a brand as an asset which can be sold and/or included in the balance sheet. From a marketing perspective, it is customer brand equity, or brand strength in the market.

Positive & Negative Brand Equity

Positive brand equity is the positive effect of the brand on the difference between the prices that the consumer is willing to pay for the brand known in comparison to the value of the benefit derived. Positive brand equity is created by marketing activities such as advertising, PR, and promotional activity. Negative brand equity can exist due to catastrophic events and negative customer experiences associated with the brand.

The most elementary part of a brand to achieve positive brand equity is the brand name. A brand name can convey much about the brand itself, particularly a brand name that is easy to remember and recall. The brand name could be suggestive, for example, Chicken Inn. The brand name itself is sufficient in conveying that for chicken, Chicken Inn is the brand.

Components of Brand Equity

There are four basic components that constitute brand equity. They are *brand awareness, brand association, brand quality, and brand loyalty.*

Dimensions and Items & Description

1. **Brand Awareness**
   Customers are very familiar with the brand
   The brand is visually appealing
   The brand represents channel cooperation
   Customers are aware of the brand when they go shopping

Powerful brands enjoy high level of consumer brand awareness which translates to the ability of potential buyers to recognize and recall the brand as a member of a certain product category. Brands which consumers are aware of enter the consideration set for possible purchase and influence the selection of products from the consideration set.

2. **Brand Association**

   When the brand offers other product categories, customers will buy it.
   Customers can easily identify the advantage of the brand.
   Customers can recognize the brand.
   The brand is different from others.

This is the relative strength of a consumer's positive feelings towards a brand, synonymous with consumers establishing and constructing an emotional bond with the brand. Consumers build relationships with brands through direct and indirect experience. Associations can be symbolic meanings, functional consequences, and attributes. Consumers associate with a service or product.

3. **Brand Quality**

   The brand is good enough to respond to customer requests for quality.
   Consumers receive the same quality as national brands.
   The brand tells customers exactly what quality will be delivered.

Perceived quality is perception/judgment as defined by the consumer about a product's overall excellence or superiority. It is critical not to lose brand equity by launching sub-standard products, powerful brands are developed through consistent and positive customer experiences over time, and this is achieved through channels, product, environment, staff behavior and communications which make the brand tangible to the consumer.

4. **Brand Loyalty**

   Customers have a good perception of the value of merchandise at stores.
   If other producers of goods/services mark down their prices customers
   Will, buy from you.
   Customers are likely to recommend your brand to others.

This is a deeply held commitment to repurchase or repatrionize a product or service consistently in the future, despite situational influences and marketing efforts that cause switching behavior. Loyalty develops via brand usage and is often characterized by a favorable attitude toward a brand and repeated purchase.

Exogenous and Endogenous variables:

Exogenous variables are extrinsic variables such as product quality, selling price, presentation and packaging. Endogenous or intrinsic variables are factors expressed by loyalty, awareness, association, quality perception and the decision to buy or rebuy.

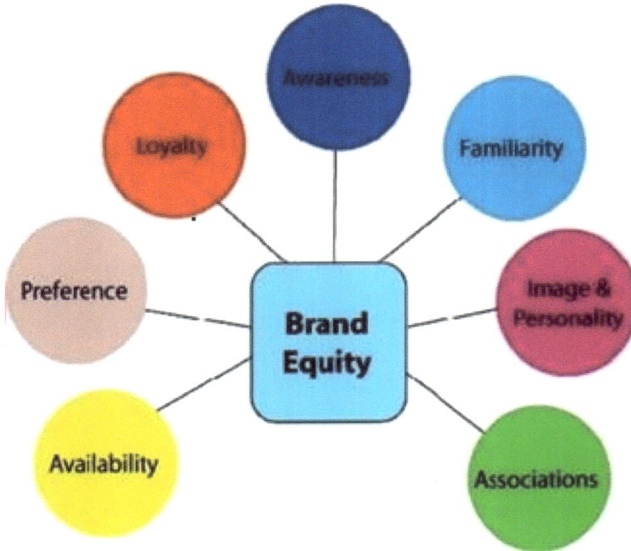

Brand Equity Model, Brandt and Johnson.

Brand Extensions

Brand extensions leverage the strengths of the existing brand by entering into new product categories by new product development. The positive image and strength of the existing brand are leveraged. Brand extensions are a means of attaining integrated brand architecture. Extensions will increase the rate of acceptance of new products and positively influences the purchase intention of consumers. This comes with efficiencies on advertising and promotion expenditures at the same time creating new market segments.

Brand extension is a common strategy deployed to increase brand equity. Existing brand equity allows companies to reduce risks and costs of launching new products, increasing sales/profits, market share, and enabling them to charge a premium price. Extensions may also enhance and facilitate a brand's awareness, increase the consumer perceived value of the brand, widen a brand's attributes and add value to a brand.

For successful brand extension consumers have to be able to expand the scope of the brand's image and information cues and other areas. Suppliers have to be able to increase the number of consumers that will accept the image and/or information function of the extension. Richard Branson's, Virgin Group, flies high in the skies of brand extension by simply attaching the name Virgin in every product they market with so diverse categories. Founded in the 1970s as a mail order record company, Virgin now has more than 200 individual companies with over $5 billion in turnover.

Line Extensions

This is sometimes confused with brand extensions. Line extensions offer new products under the same brand name, in the same product category.

Most brand extensions occur as line extensions which use existing brand names and products and extend them into new sizes, flavors, ingredients, in the existing product category. Category extensions involve higher risk as both new and existing customers are motivated to buy very different products created for existing brand names and extended new product categories. Introduction costs are higher than line extensions due to intermediaries and consumer unfamiliarity with the product, which results in increased marketing and communications expenditures and distribution channels cost.

Tips on Effective Branding
This chapter will help you by giving:

1. Practical and effective branding tips

Build a Unique Brand

Building a unique brand is a difficult process. The difficulty is not as much to, perfect strategy as to be focused, differentiated, and consistent everywhere, every time. Ensure that you deliver a consistent brand message at each customer contact point from service superiority, product, to advertising, to merchandising, distribution, and internet image just to name a few.

Create Brand Differentiation

As competition increases, brands are playing an ever increasing role in business strategy. Creating simple but powerful differentiation in the minds of key stakeholders requires a clear and compelling brand vision that expresses everything an organization does, from product to service, through environments, to the people hired and the way the organization communicates about itself.

Branding Involves Everyone

Branding is too important to be left to subject matter experts, specialists, and marketers alone. Branding involves everyone and the organizational architecture should be inclusive, participative, and totally customer-centric. The successful implementation of brand strategy is the responsibility of everyone in the organization.

Make Sure Your Research Is Thorough

Branding creates a fixed image in the minds of potential customers and part of that image relates to the products or services you sell, your level of service, and quality or value. This is why it is important to conduct thorough research and it may be necessary to solicit services from a reputable branding house or consultancy. Will this fixed image create a hindrance for you should you want to diversify your offering is something you have to consider.

Your Brand Should Establish an Emotional Connection with Your Customer

Your brand should connect you emotionally with your customer. This branding technique will cause your brand to resonate with your target audience so people emotionally connect with your brand while you ensure that you at minimum meet and preferably exceed customer expectations.

Build a Customer-Centric Brand

Know your customer needs and wants, values, and definition of quality. Cultivating your brand is a process of managing brands as an asset which begins with understanding the brand from the perspective of customers, prospective customers, and other stakeholders.

Brand Image

Strong brands project an image of a large and established business. People usually associate branding with larger businesses that have money to spend on advertising and promotion. Pay close attention to projecting the right image. Coordinate a single look across everything you do, including logo, website, brochures, ads, signage, uniforms, etc...

Create a Distinctive Logo

Create a distinctive logo to make your brand more memorable. Create a symbol or image that will differentiate you from your competitors. Key to logo design will be simplicity and lack of clutter, after all simplicity is the new sophistication. Think of Apple, they use a clean and well balanced graphic design. Use one or two basic colors that go well together

Communication Strategy

Create a communication strategy that raises targeted customers awareness and persuades customers to buy your product. Use sound judgment when analyzing issues, as you educate people via your selected communications mediums. You have to communicate effectively.

Think Strategically

Think strategically to create strategic advantage, competitive advantage, and build customer loyalty

Brand from the Inside Out

Strong brands are created from the inside out. They align with the business strategy and promote values and competencies with which external audiences want to be associated with.

Cultural Relevance

Successful brands are culturally relevant. They are in touch with the ideas, issues, and sensibilities that influence their audience's decisions. They resonate with the customer's cultural reality.

Brands Must Deliver Clarity of Difference

Compelling brands deliver clarity of difference. They know what makes them unique and communicate a point of view. Even if imitation is part of your brand strategy you are not exonerated from the responsibility of delivering clarity of difference.

Personal Branding

Personal branding should be homogenous with who you are essentially as a person. Its inception, genesis and what it metamorphosis's into should be congruent and synonymous with your personal vision, values, competencies, and what gives you fulfillment in doing. If there is a disparity or divergence it requires synchronization immediately. Your lifestyle is your brand. Essentially personal branding is the process of deliberately managing and effectively communicating who you are as a holistic person in word and deed in the dynamic and complex environments of your spatio-temporal socio, economic, political, and cultural reality.

Concluding Thoughts

Brand It or Lose It!

Inevitably you will lose market share or fail to penetrate markets if your brand and company are not customer-centric. Your task is to build a customer-centric brand and organization. Management in a customer-centric organization is a discipline of action that holistically integrates all the corporate functions to deliver systematic value to customers beyond their expectation. Whether you are engaged in the developmental stages of branding, managing your brand, rebranding, or implementing your brand strategy you have to ensure that at each expression of branding that those activities are customer-focused. Failure to do so and market share will decline and be lost to the competition. Failure to do so means you are not branding it and losing market share (current and future).

Branding steps have a significant impact on revenues without the need for big budgets, such as the brand positioning strategy, the naming of a product, the packaging design, the delivery process of a service, the consistency of the brand experience at each contact with the customer, to consider a few.

Remember! Your brand is your promise to your customer. It tells them what they can expect from your products and services, and it differentiates your offering from your competitors. Your brand is derived from who you are, who you want to be, and who people perceive you to be – build a reputable REPUTATION.

Execution: Brand It Or Die!

It would be interesting to see the results of an organization that utilized branding as a basic or core strategy. The late Peter Drucker argued once that organizations should consider adopting marketing as a basic strategy. The logic being that organizations have developed mastery at the financial management, product development, quality management, production and operations management, but they had not developed competency in the area of marketing. Can the same logic not be borrowed, for organizations that have resolved matters of price, place, product, and promotion; could branding not be the missing link between the firm and its consumer? It is not your adopted brand philosophy that will achieve the desired results, nor is it its verbal or documented articulation, results are the result of deliberate and efficacious execution, it's all about execution. You can have the most eloquent brand philosophy, plan, and strategy but without execution it is not worth the paper it is written on.

Brand It Or Die! Live The Brand

You have a choice. How consistently you present your brand will either strengthen the company or weaken it, this is contingent upon how you "live the brand." The brand experience is strengthened and consolidated when it is instilled into all your products and services, at every customer touch point including packaging, logos, your tagline, your corporate culture, and in employee training. The brand experience is weakened when it is ignored, or worse, through inconsistent usage, mixed messages, uncaring attitudes, and impatience. Every employee has the responsibility to be a steward of the brand.

Your customer's notion of your brand is formed from his or her first experience or "imprint" with your company or with your products or services at customer touch points. Every customer interaction is a valuable opportunity to enrich the brand.

With your new brand strategy in place, you can begin integrating it into all your marketing and communications efforts and activities, everything you do and are, and watch the effectiveness and efficiency of your branding, business, and marketing efforts soar.

Finally, deliver superior brand experience.

Bibliography

Copeland, John T., *Successful Brand Repositioning,* McKinsey & Company, http://marketing.mckinsey.com (2001)

Drucker, Peter F., (2001), *The Essential Drucker*, HarperCollins Publishers Inc., 10 East 53rd Street, New York, NY 10022

Ehlers, Tienie, and Lazenby, Kobus, *Strategic Management: Southern African Concepts and Cases*, Van Schaik Publishers, Hatfield, Pretoria, South Africa

Global Entrepreneurship Monitor Uganda, (2004), *"Executive Report"* Makerere University Business School

Longenecker, Justin; Moore, Carlos; and Petty, William, *Small Business Management: An Entrepreneurial Emphasis*, South-Western College Publishing, Cincinnati, Ohio, USA

Muyimba, N.K.A, *Brand Orientation, Brand Distinctiveness and SME Performance In Uganda,* Conference proceedings of the Second Annual International Conference On Entrepreneurship (SAICE), Wits Business School, South Africa, October 2009

O' Brien, Virginia, *The Fast Forward MBA in Business "Tough ideas made easy"*, John Wiley & Sons, Inc, USA

Phillips, Carol., (2005) *Branding From The Inside Out: How To Approach Brand Strategy, Brand Measurements and The Management of Brands As Assets*, BrandAmplitude, LLC

Smit, P; Cronje; G, Brevis, T; and Vrba, M, *Management Principles: A Contemporary Edition For Africa,* Juta & Co, Cape Town, South Africa

Stegemann, Nicole, *Unique Brand Extension Challenges For Luxury Brands*, University of Western Sydney, Australia (10/2006)

Thompson, Chris, (2005) *Advertising In Zimbabwe*

Pangolin Corporate Training & Development

2 Tall Trees Lane, Philadelphia, Borrowdale, Harare
0734 405 858, 0773 288 450, 0777 775 252

We derive our vision and mission from providing world-class learning and development programs. Our fulfilment emanates from helping businesses develop more efficient and cost-effective training solutions, to produce tangible, sustainable, and long-term results.

Today's world is in constant change. To satisfy the market's need for innovation, originality, and demand for better products and services, training becomes an extremely important aspect of an organization's and individual's career, regardless of qualification or experience.

At PCTD we use our expertise to define, measure, and develop the capabilities needed to make organizations successful by growing the talents of their people, improving customer relationships, and increasing organizational performance. Quality training to our clients is our primary objective.

For further information on our products or services write PCTD at 2 Tall Trees Lane, Borrowdale, Harare or call us on +263 734 405 858 or +263 777 775 252.

BrandHouse

BrandHouse is PCTD's sister company. Our duty is to assist brands gain relevance and provide deep value to their customers. As brand consultants our objective is to help you develop a strong brand, influence the buying decisions and shape perceptions held by customers. Our team of specialists generate client satisfaction through genuine partnership, sound advice, great service and products, and high quality creative solutions.

We deliver effective designs to assist you improve your customer connection, your competitiveness, and the image of your product or service. We guarantee tangible results at an affordable price.

Our portfolio offers high quality creative and effective services which include branding, rebranding, corporate identity, marketing collateral, brand packaging design, graphic and web design, PR, advertising, and corporate printing.

For further information on our products or services write BrandHouse at 2 Tall Trees Lane, Borrowdale, Harare or call us on +263 777 775 252 or +263 734 405 858.

www.ingramcontent.com/pod-product-compliance
Lightning Source LLC
Chambersburg PA
CBHW041720200326

41521CB00001B/134